Ol' Lady House

By Dee Collins

Illustrated by Pari Collins

DEDICATION

To my family,
who taught me that it's not the house,
but the love poured into it
that makes it a home.

Little Ol' Lady, I call my house, oh,
how I love her so!

Well-worn and repaired, throughout the years, is the
only way I know.

Decade by decade she gives so much,

a covering of warmth, a place of trust.

I blanket her lines
with spackle and paste,
hoping her age fades with
mortar and paint.

Her floorboards move,
just a slight foundation slip,
but time-worn wood
becomes her benefit.

She moans out loud when the
weather challenges her,
"Stand up straight!"

And, when she musters up the
courage, we all celebrate!

Some of her windows don't
work as before, but a few greasy rubs,
and voila, all is restored!

Her battered places tell a story,

her drywall just a tad dry,

but charming wallpaper covers

and she's beautified.

I wonder, sometimes,
how often her doors have been
slammed,

 cups of hot coffee spilled,

 and breakfast toast
made with jam.

 Oh, some might say her cracks are too deep, bulldoze her down she ain't worth the keep!

But, In the evening, after a long
moonwalk, I sit on her stoop, and
time slows the tick-tock.

I admire her neighborly friends near and far, she
has known them as long as the motorcar.

On the days when the sun lights up Ol' Lady House and the cool breeze whistles away,

her shutters just smile,
the sweet roses sing,
and House has something to say.

"Thank you for taking care
of me," she says,

"my bones are no longer young.
But my spirit is strong, many years I have left,
Ol' Lady is my name for home."

About The Author

Dee Collins is a missionary
who enjoys meeting people, discovering beauty
in unfamiliar places, and writing about it all.

Whether she's thrifting, gardening,
or learning something new, she embraces
each season and
the opportunities God provides.

About The Illustrator

Pari Collins is an animator and illustrator.
She enjoys animals, horticulture, writing, and toy collecting.

She loves visual narrative collaboration and working on animated films, video-game animation, and illustrations.

You can find her on an day curled up with her cat and a good book.

Made in the USA
Columbia, SC
11 April 2025

56478854R00015